COCKTAILS AT THE MAUSOLEUM

Also by Susan Musgrave:

Songs of the Sea-Witch   1970
Entrance of the Celebrant   1972
Grave-Dirt and Selected Strawberries   1973
The Impstone   1976
Selected Strawberries and Other Poems   1977
Becky Swan's Book   1977
Kiskatinaw Songs (with Sean Virgo)   1979
A Man to Marry, A Man to Bury   1979
Tarts and Muggers: Poems New and Selected   1982

FOR CHILDREN:

Gullband (illustrated by Rikki)   1974
Hag Head (illustrated by Carol Evans)   1980

FICTION:

The Charcoal Burners   1980

Susan Musgrave
Cocktails at the Mausoleum

McClelland and Stewart

The Canadian Publishers
McClelland and Stewart Limited
25 Hollinger Road, Toronto M4B 3G2

Canadian Cataloguing in Publication Data

Musgrave, Susan, 1951–
  Cocktails at the mausoleum

Poems.
ISBN 0–7710–6651–1

I. Title.

PS8576.U8C62 1985   C811'.54   C85–098241–3
PR9199.3.M84C62 1985

The publisher makes grateful acknowledgment to
the Ontario Arts Council and the Canada Council
for their assistance.

Set in Perpetua by The Typeworks, Vancouver
Printed and bound in Canada by Gagné Ltd.

FOR YOU, LITTLE BOOTS

CONTENTS

III: "WE COME THIS WAY BUT ONCE"

IV: REQUIEM FOR TALUNKWUN ISLAND

QUEEN CHARLOTTE ISLAND POEMS

V: SLEEPING TOGETHER

VI: MY BOOTS DRIVE OFF IN A CADILLAC

I

COMING INTO TOWN, COLD

The night is cool.
Love takes us and changes us
so that even the moon is always
rising – it rises behind your eyes
where I see things enter and grow.
There is a light around your body,
a pale delicate light that makes
everything seem brighter.
It's a strange light and at times
it makes touching you impossible.

I touch you.
The light comes from inside you,
from a place that even the moon
cannot reach. You pull me there
with all your knowledge of darkness.
I come, I stay. In this light
I could easily be blinded.

I know that. So sometimes when
we touch I start to feel afraid.
You know it too, and cover up my eyes,
but the moon shines through your skin
and I feel it enter me.
I am surprised; I have never shared
this moon with anyone. Later,
much later, you give me the whole sky.

and we headed for the foothills
on a greyhound bus. It was hot,
there was nothing to say. We hadn't
even planned to come this way together.

Years ago I made the same journey
from Sacramento into the foothills
looking for adventure. I was thirteen
and that summer my godmother taught me
how to cook. I wanted to pan for gold
instead, run wild into the mountains.

I remember deep pools in a clear
mountain stream, and lying beside a boy
who said he loved me too much.
We didn't touch, he loved me that much.
I ached, I wanted him all afternoon.

Afterwards I confessed, confused by my
feelings. My godmother said I was oversexed;
all summer long I went on needing.

I think you must have been with me then,
I think you have always been with me.
There's something of you in everyone
I've loved. There's something in you
that's different.

If this bus stops anywhere, we'll get out.
You say you want to see dolphins as the
desert rolls past. I've got sand in my eyes
and sometimes I can taste water. The desert
is an ocean, and the waves go by unbroken.

You take my hand. Your face – I've been
watching it secretly for hours – turns
towards me and you bend to kiss me.
It's the first time we've touched;
the surf breaks in my blood.

I half-believe we could travel forever,
gazing out through tinted glass and
breathing the salt breeze. The breeze
is gentle; I think I can hear dolphins.
You move your body closer.
I think I can hear them singing.

and Paul is in Acapulco
looking for avocados.
Papayas and mangoes are ripening
in the shade; when the moon is this way
we each have hidden powers.

There are frogs in the underworld
singing of the upper air. They
want to go there, they want to
dress in women's bodies and
come to our bed bringing messages
from the spirits.

The bed is cold. Paul is in
Acapulco. Strange beautiful women
are trailing him through the streets—
they know he's not ordinary,
they want to know more about him.

They enter my sleep, like frogs,
like spirit beings; later when I wake
I don't know who I am.
The women are hungry, they wrap
their tongues around me. Their eyes
are the colour of the Acapulco moon,
their skin is like Paul's avocados.

Later we laugh about it, how
Paul was followed home and the bed
filled up with frogs. Still I'm confused;
I think those frogs were human.
Frogs wouldn't look at Paul
that way, like hot-blooded women
in town for a good time.

that is, not knowing anyone
and having nowhere to go,
not speaking the foreign language either
but trying to get by on hard-earned
Canadian poetry royalties.

Miami was a disaster. I lost
my pen and my American Express Card
(one an omen, the other an inconvenience).

Paul says I shouldn't be superstitious
but he's not here right now. It's mystical
out there where he is. I would quit tomorrow
but there is still his body to be reckoned with.

I'm glad I'm not in Miami
though I slept through most of the week.
There's no place for poetry in a world
like that, and furthermore I met no one
who'd even heard of Vancouver.

In Panama I'll learn Spanish
and soon I'll have someone to talk to.
An address, maybe, where friends can write,
and one day a house with a view to
South America.

Nothing is ever enough– the thought
creates panic. I'm over twenty-nine and
only inertia stops me from considering suicide.

Paul, if he were here, would provide another
reason. When we're naked or just rising
half-naked above the bed, I can't even remember
which continent we've left.

in your white suit
and your python boots

leaving you there and driving home
in the old vw
with the accelerator pedal sticking.

Rain comes through the floor
there's no more I can do

giving and taking,
just getting through.

But you are out of my arms
and into another airport–
I want to hold you and bring you
back down, back into my arms,
down to the ground.

Your love is safe with me,
I want you to know.
When you leave take me with you–
let me go.

supposing you have no one.
Supposing the person you love is in
Panama, has been away for weeks
and you don't know how to find him.

At night in the house all things are crying–
the tea-pot, the clock-radio, the things
you rely on. The mirror stares back at you
from a distance that makes breathing impossible.
You see nothing but empty shadows, and these
have the faces of strangers.

Supposing you go to town, you meet and
talk with friends but they too have become
strangers. Your family invites you home
but when you arrive they no longer know you.
Supposing, later, when you drive down the
highway, even your own house has abandoned you.

Supposing this happens when you are
twenty-nine; supposing it happens this way.
All your life you have never belonged
and suddenly you are nowhere.

You pull up your favourite chair, you sit
alone in the garden. You count, very slowly,
the number of times your heart beats in a minute
– supposing it beats forever in the emptiness
of your body? Supposing you stop counting and
no one is there to notice. Supposing then
that the one person who might have cared
comes walking towards you, hangs his head
and is silent.

MY PIRATE CAME BACK FROM BOGOTA
WITH POWDER-BURNS ON HIS LEG

and a .38 in his briefcase
and a pocketful of lead.

Afterwards we drank orange juice
and talked about emeralds

there was a moon, I remember,
a cold slit in the sky,
and a war going on in Ecuador
and another in Guatemala.

Later, tired of talking,
we made love. I think it was
on the roof of the Hotel
Conquistador, I think it was
all we had left to do
given the night and the
thin moon which, when fatter,
lacks the same power.

You pressed yourself into me,
tired of living alone.
There comes a time when you
tire of a life together,
but that comes later still.

I remember I was thinking
how longing becomes regret
when you pressed yourself so hard
that a bullet bore into me.
It left an impression on the
inside of my thigh, as below me

in the doorway a blonde girl
kissed a black man goodbye.

She had her face turned
upwards to the sky where her
eyes burned like my trigger-hand
to pull and unload the
murderer in the heart.

You held on to me as if you thought
love could last forever.
The blonde girl left with her
poodle in a cab.

HUNCHBACK ON THE BUGA ROAD

Stopping beside a place where the
pine trees grew wild and straight as
children, I saw her cower and shrink
from the flowers in the ditches
as if she knew beauty
was something to be ashamed of.

I saw her face.
The children who came out of nowhere
tried to step on her shadow;
it was good luck, they told us,
to step on the hump.

She was singing a small song,
of possibilities and roads not
taken. Of laughter and clear nights
and a man she had somewhere forgotten.

At least I thought that's what
she sang. Out of her sight we
stopped for a picnic, and picked flowers
that were too beautiful. They died
in the trunk of the car that night.

In Buga. We made love under
a clear sky, in the shadow of the Andes,
and afterwards I started singing–
do you remember how you used to laugh?
I sang the old woman's song again,
at least I think I was singing.

No matter; it was years ago.
I've learned to speak her language and
I know now what she was saying. She sang
"Can't reach where it itches." Only that.
I wish, at the time, you had told me.

CALI

Wind comes through the canyon,
a soft wind with
no name or direction.
It lights upon your eyes like
wakening birds

and love, once something so small
and ordinary, touches me.

SIR LIONEL LUCKHOO, LISTED IN THE GUINNESS BOOK OF RECORDS AS THE WORLD'S MOST SUCCESSFUL ADVOCATE WITH 228 SUCCESSIVE MURDER ACQUITTALS, HUMBLY LAYS HIS ALL AT THE FEET OF JESUS

There I stood in the rain
black skirt hitched up high and a
hint of lace at the neckline when someone,
Jesus it seems, smiled down on me,
opened his large good arms and
offered me his deckchair under the tarpaulin.

I walked up to that deckchair
with little faith in anything,
quite ready to turn my back on life completely
but fearing the inexorable conclusion.

I admit I was impressed by his
impeccable manners, old heart-throb he
with teeth flashing.
Like daggers of bone, that smile hit home—
he was a shark feeding on cool wedges of
sunset and dark eyes flashing under the jacaranda.

I admit I was feeling divided –
the fish of my flesh could easily have fed a
multitude – when Sir Lionel arrived in his
chauffeur-driven Mazda.
Jesus skipped the reception line to mix with the
common people while I sat there watching,
confused by a spectacle that others seemed
to be taking for granted– the crippled rising up
and dancing, the blind unbandaging the injured.

Wine flowed like blood from the throats of the
flowers while birds sang from the trees.
The sun and the moon shone at once in the

same sky, and all the stars became butterflies,
frail and dazzling.

Sir Lionel looked amazed; he quickly adjusted
his cufflinks.
When his voice was raised his words were barely
audible; for the first time in his life he had to
compete for an audience.

But when the dust had settled over all the
bright dancers, and the stars were only stars
again in a sky that loomed over us as if in
final judgment, Sir Lionel led the crowd
in prayer, and left shortly afterwards
with Jesus in the Mazda.

The crowd followed.
So much for me, all sudsy heart and soul—
I was left sitting there.
I had to make my own way home:
the way was clear and I went alone.

After two years of torture, he said,
he couldn't touch a book of poetry
without trembling
They let him go because he was the
wrong person– after two years of torture
he could not say *I love you*
to his wife or his children.

His torturers, he said, were
ordinary people– they had feelings too.
Sometimes they would show him photographs
of their families– ordinary people
like me, like you.

Personally I do not like to
think about torture. I do not like to
hear of it on the radio, or read about it
or even believe it happens.
I know it happens.
He told me, after two years of torture
you still can't believe it's happening.

You just want to die but
they won't let you. If you happen to die
they have a real sense of loss.
Torturers, he said, have feelings too.
They are ordinary people
like me, like you.

No one can shut out
the shamelessness of the body,
or love the discipline of torture
and remain faithful.

No one can shut out
the sadness of the body,
the need of desire
to grow and rot.

Every time it is the same
thing, always the scales tip
for the innocence of guilt.
Always I have no curative powers.

I am the bride with
worms around her heart
and a skull bursting with goodness
like a church goblet.
I am the bearer of accused children.

No gallantry can ease
the painfulness of the body
or understand the camouflage
to celebrate its loss.

Death is nakedness
suddenly become flesh.
Suicide is pornography.

helicopters, too, over the
Bridge of the Americas.
Where the sky bends it bleeds,
meets shark-infested water.
We make love at the water's edge,
ignoring the dead soldiers.

They grow stiff inside their
duty pants, their heads picked
clean as bullets. We could
plant flowers in this difficult
spring, affirm our belief in
something beyond the future.

At least it doesn't rain here
like it does in the country we've
come from. At least we have
each other to hold, though how
through this pain can
loving keep us together?

Like hurt birds in a cage
we learn to accept the loss.
It's safer to stay
where the vulture is only an image.

For the planes descend and the
love goes out of us.
From where we are lying we can
sense their fear– it drives us
into our own bodies and
there we become strangers.

We are tired, too, and the tide
has risen beyond us. We embrace
as if it's not happened before,
a hopeless conceit, but human.

out of the water onto the
beach, a freak marriage of
flesh and air with terror
a gimmick to capture the
crowd's attention.

I was just sitting there
with various organs missing,
an oddity myself
having so far managed to
appear quite ordinary

when the shark singled me
out, sliced through the
heart's cavity, through the
hole, that is, where pieces
of my heart were missing.

But oh I had teeth too
and a weird thirst for my
own blood, and there was
nothing that shark knew
I didn't know better.

We conspired and soon
we rolled up the rug;
athlete and intellect
we had that beach crawling.

I suppose it's an art,
the act of maiming,
and for one complete moment
I felt like a creator.

Then the crying began
and the terrible craziness.
I stayed while the shark swam
away; the art of survival was
something he understood better.

But the dying wanted reasons
where the grave was reason enough
and all I could do was to toast the
shark as the mob moved in to
reconcile our differences.

The sad event would alter
nothing– no laws or fears or
complicated griefs. They dragged
my body onwards to the sea.
The shark came to greet me
cradling his oily genitals.

II

SECOND SIGHT

I am the girl in gazelle horns
and a torn nightdress.
I have no body.
See, nothing hurts.

Yesterday it snowed.
I lay down making a large good angel.

Today it thawed.
Another looking out through her small
blind eyes, crying

whose horns are those,
whose torn clothes?

SECOND SIGHT

For Marilyn

The flies were thick in the bush
and we had nothing but trouble.

Our clothes were uncomfortable;
like sleepwalkers we stripped
and spread wide our arms

it was misty and cool

our eyes could not focus on
details

and everywhere the smell of the
wild, wild roses
assaulted our senses.

We found a clearing and built a
fire.
We were two little sisters
and life together was awesome.

Being born into that wide, cool,
misty, wild rose morning

we touched each other and a
bear came.
A bear came running with a crowd
after him,
a black bear with a secret black hole
in his heart.

We wanted to help.
Two sisters we believed in sharing

and called him to our human fire,
content with caring.

He was an ugly bear, unused to
kindness.
He did not forgive us
but embraced us.

Two old gaping women we
still remember that touch

and try to recall the vision
in words:

an old bear echoes
enough, enough!

I took a wire cage into the woods
in which to sit and watch the animals.
They gathered round me as I'd hoped they would
and sat, expressionless, with closed eyes,
warming themselves in the sun.

Their bodies were beautiful, unlike mine;
their bodies were solitary, never lonely.
They must have sat for hours in one place
as if to reassure me all was understood.

Their patience was exhausting. All night
I watched till dark and light were
blotted out and whole seasons passed.
I did not leave that cage again but lay
under the cool influence of the stars,
awake and dreaming.

My dreams were always the same.
Always in my own image those animals rose
out of the dust, animals with human faces
whose eyes were open, sorrowful.

Their bodies were broken.
No longer content to sit and stare
at one such as this, confined by choice
within the shadows of a spectral cage,
they paced as those condemned, and wept,
while I, the guilty one, was saved.

"HE ONLY WISHES
THEY WOULD HEAR HIM SING"

Conrad is slipping away.
What can I say–
he's as good as dead
and doesn't seem to know it.

Or doesn't show it.
It happens to everyone–
soon I won't have anyone.

Richard's come from Venice
for the funeral,
Jenny from south London.
Delays, delays–
Conrad is sleeping,
he's slept all day.

His wife says, "It's time.
He really should be going."
I think she wants him to go.
He won't know the difference anyway.

He is better dead–
that's all there is to say.
No one will save him.
He won't be saved.

EAGLET TRICKS

After Ted Hughes

The first trick is being born
not easy to grasp, no,
the grip being difficult at
dizzying altitudes

the appetite hideous.

A voluptuous gluttony,
a gorging on flesh;
the eventual intimacy of
earth and death.

I guffaw.
the sky is evidence of my unalterable existence,
my leavings are a different matter
my judgment, law.

Unarguable I ascend
all wingbone and talon,
a flick of a bird only
the quirk of a cranky brain.

The trick is old,
the art unaccountable and infinite.

The blood moves sluggishly
through a drudgery of veins
till death, infective,
replaces pain with dull efficiency.

Today I found a severed head
lying beside a tree. The tree
had been cut down it seemed
by someone who came to me in a dream.
She said she had nowhere to live
anymore. She looked like me.

Where does a person go, I mean
after losing her head that way.
The tree was my favourite, and
as a child,
I could climb higher than anyone.

BLACK MUMMY

has a hairy belly
a snatch made of jelly
a chest full of surprises.

Black Mummy has a gorilla
his name is Goliath
he lives up inside her
he catches spiders.

Black Mummy has a greedy pussy
it's very juicy
it's a blackberry pussy.

Black Mummy has a dolly
it looks like me
it has no body
it's a funny dolly.

Blackberry Mummy
lives in my tummy
I have no feelings
I cry anyway.

JERUSALEM

It's a strange place to go,
but then millions do, I guess.
For two nights I've been dreaming
and dancing– flights leave every day
and something keeps whispering of it
over and over.

Think of the poor world, Jeffrey,
if only we could make the world work.
We're not the first to have felt
this way; the thing is we feel
small, not wanting to sleep but to
lie down wonderfully together

and believe in something.
I suggest Jerusalem, flights
leave every day. You say no,
think of the hordes, we don't need
a holiday, and neither of us religious.

But I was thinking of change–
only that– how to make something whole,
keep it drifting and uncertain.

You want to stay home:
it's Christmas, you say. As usual
we'll hang our stockings, side by side.
Someone, you or I, will fill them.

right under the Pope's nose
in a see-through shirt and skin-tight breeches.
You could hear the hosts of angels
arguing over the telescope, while others posed
eagerly with Instamatic cameras.

Such over-exposure! The priests put down their
pocket-books and prayed for darkness while the
nuns stood speechless and a limp hand
led the choir. The choir-boys had hot dreams
and prayed for other miracles. Sinners confessed
to unnamed crimes.

A sign of the times. Outside the gates
women of all ages tore off their hats and
unbuttoned blouses. Hem-lines became obsolete
and legs swung free as pythons. The sky itself
was dazzled and, higher up, teeth were gritted.
Breasts and buttocks made front-page spreads
and the Pope retired early to contemplate.

Angels and saints hooted– stars popped like
corks and champagne rained until all was
heavenly disorder. Tamara, in hot pink, made
mince out of the clergy. She was thinking, too,
of the boy she'd finally left, and the
heavy gold crucifix he'd given her.
She'd tossed it away while dancing, braless,
up the steps. She needed the freedom to travel.

THREE WITCHES GO FOR LUNCH IN ELORA

Driving into Waterloo on a Wednesday,
the air smells of roast pig. In Conestogo
I pass a barn that burned down during the
night, and later, in the paper, read that
five hundred pigs were killed.

Rikki and Jane saw pig-ghosts in the
sky, unfavourable omens floating like
plump ions over my office at St. Jerome's.
They saw a dead cat, too, at the side of the
road, and a crow strutting with bad news from
home, the sudden death of a friend.

This little pig stayed home.
My husband won't eat pork because once,
in Science, they left a pork chop sitting
all night in a bowl of milk. By morning
the worms had emerged, leaving the pork chop
frail as a doily. Mother said *cooking it
kills the worms*, and always overcooked the
Sunday joint.

Driving out of Waterloo with Rikki and
Jane to Elora for lunch we see them in the
distance– five hundred overcooked pigs
out for an afternoon gallop. The sky,
in fact, is full of them, fiery-eyed
insomniacs with a cold-blooded lust for women.

Hot damn says Jane.
We hoof it.

III

"WE COME THIS WAY BUT ONCE"

"WE COME THIS WAY BUT ONCE"

A poetry reading tour of England, Wales, Scotland, and Paris with
bill bissett and George Johnston, October 25–November 9, 1980

I

I don't know how they keep
this train on the tracks
the wheels turn and that's it
in two weeks
bill will be chopping wood
in the Cariboo, I'll be
down in Panama and George
back with his family.

I don't know how they keep
this train on the tracks
with all the distractions
they have to face daily.

I've been faithful to Paul
for nearly six weeks
it's not exactly easy
in fact it's a record.

I don't like sleeping alone
at night I like to hold someone.
When I start to dream about
old relationships, then it is
especially difficult.

bill says you have to wait
two years in between
major relationships
I've been waiting a few weeks
and already I'm impatient.
I don't know how they keep

this train on the tracks,
the wheels turn and
that's it.

The men along the line are
smoking, talking
bill says "in two hours
I can smoke." I don't know
how he does it.

I don't know how anyone does.
I just want to hold someone and
right now it's not possible
it never is when you
really want to   there is no one
there is really no one.

The wheels turn and
that's it   the train
stays upright, it's designed
like this.

The men along the line
are hunched against the cold
I watch them   they watch me
Mrs. Jackson says the cold is
piercing.

Yesterday at church I got
a message on my palm;
bill saw it and touched it.
bill got a message, too;
Mrs. Peel, the healer, saw
a question in his life.

In Vancouver one time I saw
a question mark on the mountain.
I was upstairs holding some
TV personality, my life

was on the line, I changed,
that was it

there clearly was, that day,
a question mark on the mountain,
and now on my palm, and in
bill's life.

But last night when we talked
I wrapped myself in his words
and there I wasn't cold anymore
I wasn't scared or lonely.

Later I had a dream– we moved to
Arizona. bill and I could actually
go there; George, of course, could
bring his large good family.

II

In yellow Wellingtons I went
to Sylvia Plath's grave
on a cold day in November–
bill was with me.

We'd heard she was buried in
unconsecrated ground
it's all the same now, the vicar
told us   he hadn't known her
personally.

At first we couldn't find her–
the cold was making it hard.
Maybe she did it to get warm
bill said. That must have been part of it.

I found a blue suitcase
in among the weeds–
someone had lost it or
left it behind, no doubt
a worn-out traveller. I too
would like to get rid of some
weight. I carry so much with me
and most of it unnecessary.

The grave was wild, I guess
that's good. I would not choose
a tidy grave myself– nor any grave:
the day will come when I have
no choice.

It's all the same now
standing at the grave's edge
bill with the blue suitcase
packed and matching the

blue shoes he'd worn out
with so much travelling.

We sat for hours in a pub
away from the cold and talked
of unrelated things. By that
I mean we avoided love or grief.

And high above Heptonstall
a cold moon hung in the sky,
a blonde thing with a yellow rose
in its side   a funny duchess
a suicide.

III

The time I like best is
when we are alone and talking

this isn't a romance
so it's all right to laugh

I don't think I laughed once
all summer in Mexico
I didn't talk much either.
Lovers are quite serious, you say.
I agree, it's curious.

And complicated sometimes.
One woman you knew had herself
sterilized   I wonder
if that simplified anything
or simply hurt

we hide our hurt well
but this isn't a romance.

If it were a romance
and you brushed against me
the way you do now, in
friendship, it would probably
mean something. If I
waited for you to call and
you didn't, it would probably
hurt and I *wouldn't* hide it.

This isn't a romance.

Not laughing gets serious
sometimes   for instance
when you are leaving someone
or they are leaving

I mean people are always
leaving   next week
so will you

but it's all right to laugh
it's all right to laugh.

IV

The silver bracelet
bill didn't get
is still in the window

I dreamed of it again last night
I had wanted to buy it for
him and he for someone else
isn't that always how it is
I mean   as long as you live
your case is very doubtful.

You decide, say, not to live.
You think you are dying to
punish someone when really
you are dying to free them

that's a good enough reason
for staying alive

and all this over one
silver bracelet.

The bracelet was in the window
of a shop owned by Mr. Benson.
His neighbour told us he was
never open. They no longer speak:
Mr. Benson, she said, is a bit
of a twister.

We might find him at the library
where he goes to read the news.
"A single sentence will suffice
for modern man: he fornicated
and he read the papers."

That's our Mr. Benson. Hot on
his trail we high-tailed it

down to the library. He was late,
it wasn't like him, said the
librarian. He wore a beard and a
black cloak– his grandfather
was a warlock.

bill searched every café (George
took the 9:06 up to Newcastle).
I thought perhaps Mr. Benson
was in bed, having overslept
or died– the ultimate sentence.

But we found him walking back
to open up his shop   he never
opened before noon he said,
but for the silver bracelet
one hundred and fifty pounds

sterling! bill was prepared to
pay around thirty   I would have
gone higher and given it to him
so that he, in turn, could
give it as a gift

but things don't actually work
like this– my case would still
have been doubtful.

The silver bracelet
bill didn't get
will always be in that window

on it a young girl and a
man who is also unattainable.

They do not touch though their
fates are intertwined.   Together
they shine   in bill's eye,
in mine.

V

"I heard some good news today,"
said George. "We come this way
but once." We were on a train
between London and Brighton—
I seemed to remember having
come this way before.

It was ten years ago and the
circumstances were similar.
I was waiting to meet a man
on whom all my life depended.
He was late, I recall, or else he
never arrived. Years later I can't say
it makes any difference.

I am still waiting, there is
still no one. In the station at
Brighton I heard George Harrison sing
"I really want to see you but it
takes so long..."

Last night in Oxford I dreamed
I went blind. I was high up in the
sky; as usual I was waiting for
someone. Whoever it was arrived
but then I couldn't see him.
bill dreamed our ship was about to
go down. George dreamed, blissfully,
nothing.

In my life my dreams are the
only continuity   bill the same
though I can't speak for him.

I suspect as much   when the ship
sank he stayed with it. I, too,
though floundering. Others, around
us, abandoned the ship and drowned.

VI

The terrible parting in
Paris or London has yet
to come, with all the sadness
rolled into one

but you can't hedge on the wheel.

Today we're together in
Glasgow. It's starting to feel
permanent; all the hotels,
the lonely stations, they're
starting to feel familiar.

In Norwich I saw a church
that had been bombed by a
Zeppelin and in Coventry the
new cathedral. By Cardiff
we were thoroughly festive.

bill was kept awake in Dundee
with the election on television
and a toilet endlessly flushing

I slept through dreams of
one train pulling away after
another

we were saying goodbye
on a platform in some station
it meant we would
stop travelling together
it meant we would go on alone
and in different directions.

George had gingercake and honey
I had a handful of rain

I said what use to anyone
is a handful of rain
I am always trying
to make sense out of things.

I want everything to last,
at least to stay the same.
bill says I should let it all go
you can't hedge on the wheel.

So I turn and the wheel
turns and the sadness turns too
into tears and laughter, the
unspeakable circuit

one train pulls away after
another and all the sadness
is rolled into one.

What use is a handful of
rain I say   away with it!
Let it go!

and in every other town.
All around there were mountains,
when I looked down I saw the
mountains reflected.

I saw your face.
I must have heard your name in
every place I stopped and
each day seemed the same and
each night took me further away from you.

David stood up to read his poetry.
He said every day billions of things happen
and are forgotten. For a while
his poetry made me laugh,
but then I was alone again
in another hotel room.

I tried writing you a letter, I said
Bill it's all I can do to drag myself
upstairs. I've been bawling to adolescents
the inscrutable agonies of the dead.
In my room in this Travelodge
there are two double beds.

The letter never got finished.
I fell asleep reading a book,
reading over and over *"There's a thing
he doesn't know. He doesn't know
you can't catch the glory on a hook
and hold on to it. That when you fish for
the glory you catch the darkness too.
That if you hook twice the glory
you hook twice the fear."*

All night I slept and dreamed I was
running. There was a mountain road
and flowers so beautiful I wanted to
pick them all and press them in a book.
That way I could keep them and
they wouldn't change.
I think you were running with me.

IV

REQUIEM FOR TALUNKWUN ISLAND
QUEEN CHARLOTTE ISLAND POEMS

I WANT TO REMEMBER DAVID

I want to live on the same island
as David

I want to drive down to 'Charlotte
in his '56 Buick Special
stopping along the way to pick mint
at Miller Creek and briefly
at Jungle Beach for lamb's quarters

if they're in season

I want to wait at the Landing
while David gets the clock-radio going
and leaves the car on display at
Skidegate Esso
where neither the highest nor
any offer shall necessarily
be accepted.

I'll bring armloads of lilac from the
condemned house where we stayed once

I remember there was that
grand occasion when David did a dance,
a striptease for the Mounties who came to
search everyone:

David was a real shocker in
black pumps.

I want to remember David
drifting in a leaky skiff without oars

alone in the rain at the north end of the world
with a picnic basket full of love letters
from Christopher.

is soul-travelling on the
Tlell River
spirit-dancing up the clam-banks
looking for trouble.

Josef's ghost is reading
The Anatomy of Melancholy
mumbling about atrocities
swigging a Skidegate Cocktail.

Josef's ghost goes hunting with a six-pack,
picnics beside the Geikie under a collapsible
umbrella.

Josef's ghost spooks geese on the
muskeg, sabotages the underground
telephone cables.

Josef's ghost courts
young Janey Brown, leaves wreaths
on her worn front doorstep.

Josef's ghost glows in the dark,
frightens the daylights out of our daft Jamie.

Josef's ghost wears a yellow hardhat,
goes to I.W.A. meetings and
leaves abruptly.
Josef's ghost declares bankruptcy at the
Kaien Consumer's Credit Union.

Josef's grave is a National Monument.
Louie's Harriet gives guided tours on
local holidays.

Josef's grave is cluttered with
old wrecked engines,
it is littered with statements from
used-car dealers.

The last time I saw Josef I was sitting beside
the ditched vw

and Josef hitched a ride into Port to scrounge
spark plugs and a new battery:

he was a real genius.

and Mike Davis just back from his
holiday brings us the bad news.

Jack Miller pours another whiskey.
His old lady has left, moved to
Pouce Coupe. So far *he's* got the kid,
but there's going to be a fight.

Mike feeds the airtight,
Helen cooks the spaghetti.

"They were wiped out in a car,
I don't know how it happened."
Most likely Joanne wasn't wearing her glasses:
they'd just come from the Commune
and Brother Love says glasses are crutches.

I remember you, Vern, at Cape Ball one winter.
We swam naked in the river.
And when the time came for you, Joanne,
you too lay down naked.
Vern delivered your second baby.

Mike says your babies are safe,
they were riding in the back.
Nobody knows how it really happened.
It happened a long way from the Islands.

Helen serves the spaghetti.
That Christmas at Cape Ball we had
smoked salmon, poached that spring.
Vern, you Viking, driving your old
vw over the Cape Ball river at
high tide– you said you'd lost
three of them that way but you

kept on trying. *"A good Volksy will do
300,000 miles on one engine."* And once,
broken down in the rain, you stopped to
offer me a ride.

Your deaths bring me closer to my own.
Friends die, friends go on living.
I visit the graves of my friends,
the houses of my friends.
Mike says he felt at home in the Commune;
Jack Miller says he hasn't time to
stay for dinner.

I eat my spaghetti, silently.
I think that being alive must not
mean very much.
Between mouthfuls I leaf through
Patrick's postcard collection:
Africa, Victoria, the World Famous
Sea Lion Caves in Oregon.
Some of them I recognize– they are
written in my own handwriting.
The messages are indecipherable now,
the ink already faded.

We talk of this and that.
Jack's latest artifact and the
illegality of eagle feathers in
Idaho.

And Vern and Joanne, dead.
Outside in the stillness a mad dog barks
at his own shadow.
Mike pours the wine and there is some
good cheese for afterwards.

Outside in the trees a dead wind is rising.
We eat our spaghetti, silently.

We are happy to see each other after a
long summer. More whiskey for the glass
and Jack Miller says he may after all
have time, this time, for supper.

REQUIEM FOR TALUNKWUN ISLAND

Talunkwun Island, named after the Haida word for phosphorus,
lies in the South Moresby group of the Queen Charlotte Islands. In
recent years clear-cut logging on the steep slopes of this island has
caused massive erosion and landslides, and has made reforestation
impossible.

I

You need not think they will make such a continual noise of singing in
Skedans Creek as they used to in your previous existence.
                              – Haida mourning song

The sad ghost of a
dead art I come
down out of the mountains.
I am weak with hunger
and my hands, oh like the
cedar trees, are stumps.

The animal inside me
sniffs the breeze.
It is all lonely darkness
breathing in and out like the
sea. Over the slick rocks at the
lip of the falls I fell
back through my father's words
and into the womb of my mother.

I almost feel whole again
remembering how it was.
I could move among the trees,
embrace heaven and rock when
gods dwelt in all places
and everything was singing.

I was raven, eagle–
I flew up up up into the top
of the salmonberry bushes.
The sky was a wilder place
in those days, wider and cleaner.
I recall you could travel
just singing and flying,
with the sea all phosphorus
lighting the way below.

Now I sit and stare at
the ocean. Sometimes for days I sit
and watch. Who hears the songs
when the voices are silent?
Who remembers the great sound we used
to make, on the shores of an island
we thought would last forever.

II

What do they think they will attain by their ships
that death has not already given them?

– William Carlos Williams

The submerged rocks sleeping like
whales did not stop them,
nor the winds that beached our
canoes and sent the
kelp gulls crying inland.
We thought their sails were clouds
and how could we have known better.
The sky was overcast and black;
my old grandmother picked cloudberries
and hid them under her hat.

The ships had come to trade–
what wealth we had was little then,
and nothing now.
My mother had to go begging
that winter. A young girl she grew
quieter and older.

If my hands were good I would
carve her something – the moon
gripped in a raven's beak –
but where would I find wood enough,
or the right spirit.
I lit a fire instead and stood in the
coals. A ship sailed out
and darkness tossed the sleepers
from its hold.

I felt tears on my young face
like rain down a mountain rock.
Something was lost; I could feel it
as I followed a deer trail to the
seacoast.

It was a day's journey
but it took me all my life.
At the end I found a highway
and people living in houses.
The trees were cut down and the
land had been sold for a pittance.
The old names were gone and the
ravens, for once, were silent.

I took the eyes of an owl
and stitched them into my head.
I took the wishbone of a foetus
and pressed it into my breast.
I sailed up into the clouds
and blackened the sky with earth.
The sky would mourn, too, the way
death does, in the roots.

III

But they could die for years, for decades,
so tall their silence, and tell you nothing.
                            – Howard Nemerov

They were sacred.
Their silence was something we
lived by, not the noise of machinery
stripping the thickets.

The trees were our spirits;
they have gone into nothingness.
They have become mortal, like us;
we diminished them and they have become
human.

Eternal life is unlivable
yet men rut like fat bucks in the
bush and women go on sighing.
It's a sad thing to be lonely in the
body, but to have no body at all–
that's the loneliest.

If I had the penis bone of a bear
I would point it at that woman.
Now there are no trees left to
shelter us, and the grass where we
could have lain is withered
and unyielding.

I wish there could be forests upon
the earth again, a place for our
children to gather. I wish the trees
would return during our own lifetime,
take hold and grow that we might
live again under their silence.

Now men talk of the wood they must
carry, they speak of the weight in
tired voices. I remember a time
when the whole world was singing,
and a love that kept us bound
by things we could not know.

IV

The wind blows where it will, and you hear the sound of
it, but you do not know whence it comes or whither it
goes; so it is with every one who is born of the Spirit.

– John 3:8

They took my hands
and threw them into the ocean.
I saw them scuttle towards Skidegate
like white crabs with supernatural power.

It is sometimes necessary to sit
and say nothing,
to watch what takes shape,
and changes, out of that silence.
It is sometimes a necessary violence.

They left my skull, I suppose
it told them nothing. My eyes had seen
the rivers full of fish but now the eyes
were older and, like the rivers, empty.
The salmon have gone elsewhere to find
their origins. Like the ghosts of my
people, they have no country.

In my chest there is something that
hurts. It once was a heart
but now it's a hole and their
fingers are eager to probe it.
I cannot tell them how life is when the
soul has left it; the body does not die
but how can they know that.

They do not remember why they were born.
They only hope to find mercy.

V

SLEEPING TOGETHER

Sometimes I forget your face,
the days erase so much of what
was never possible, but is
and is somehow permanent.

You are on some road.
A telephone rings in an empty room.
Sometimes I forget your voice,
the simple things, the certainties.

Sometimes it is too clear.
There is only distance between us.
No measure of love makes distance
reducible, the miles erase
so much of what is possible.

You are on some road.
A telephone rings in an empty room.
Sometimes I am certain; you are leaving,
it is permanent. Sometimes it is simple,
it is only distance.

Nothing resolved, we set out.
It was Sunday, raining, you said
I can't know you.
I don't.
No one does.

You lived on a mountain
you tell me that much.

The mountain had a name

tell me what it was.

I slept with war
all night I slept with war once.
I did not sleep peacefully
but killed without guilt whatever it was
I needed.

There are wounds you never wake from,
wounds that lie silent under an enemy
of skin.
There are desperate wounds
that keep you alive for hours.
They stick to you for days.
You can't heal them.

There are costly tombs on the
perfect grass
and lonely flights through drunken spaces
with nothing to pray for and
no one to listen.

It's a rut.
It's drab.
I'd like to go somewhere.

I'd like to find something worth being
wounded about
and sleep without comfort forever again.

In my dream you have become
a fisherman. You are going fishing
in my sleep.
"Sharks come to light and blood,"
you whisper, as if you have always been
a fisherman. A shark surfaces beside me;
still I cannot stop dreaming.

In your dream I am a bird,
I am trapped inside your house.
I flap my wings, beat on the windows.
"My house has no roof," you say.
Still I cannot get out.

You touch me, very gently.
You want to make me happy.
You say so, over and over.
You want me to stop dreaming.

In your dream I am dead.
You have made sure of that.
Still I am stronger than you
and more confident.
My hand does not tremble as yours does
when you twist, again, the knife.

In my dream you have become an
undertaker. You are siphoning my blood
under a cold light.
"Sharks come to light and blood,"
you whisper, as if you have always been
an undertaker. Still I go on dreaming.

You touch me, very gently.
You want me to make you happy.

You want me to stop dreaming.
You say so, over and over.

A shark is swimming towards us;
still, we sleep.
"Stop dreaming," you whisper; he surfaces
beside me.
"Stop dreaming," you shiver; he nudges your
blind windows. The shark has become a bird,
like me. Trapped inside your house we are
flying, flying.

"My house has no roof," you cry,
but the shark, too, is dreaming.
Like me, he does not want to stop dreaming.
He does not want to stop dreaming.

Somewhere you are in the world
and I am not.
You let me go and I left;
having come this far
I cannot speak of the distance.

A world lies between us.
All day I talk with men whose lives
are orderly; they want to hold me but
not touch. This time last week we were
lying in your bed.

There was a map of the world
on your wall– it covered a hole, you said.
Our bodies made that world seem small
but now I am lost in it and
you are somewhere else.

I stare out the window,
I drive into town, walk around.
Life is ordinary; I write you letters.
I tell myself it is a matter of time,
I tell myself there's no urgency.

Today I found that book on boatbuilding;
tomorrow I'll buy rosewater at the market.
These are the things you wanted
and I'll send them. If they reach you
write to me, or call me long distance.

You see, the world hurts;
without you I too am lessened.
It happens when I reach for you
and no one is there.
You see there is really no one.

You are beautiful: it hurts me.
All knowledge of you is pain
and after that knowledge is nothing.

I know you.
You take me and I change.
I break from your body
make with our lonely bodies one flesh, love,
and that enough alone.

I fill up my days with you
my nights are filled up.
Something I am grows emptier
something I am holds on and will not let go.

Time passes, only just.
You are more and more beautiful: it hurts.
Each time I reach for you something is lost;
something is born again
over and over.

That's how it was.
The black pond stank
and the leaves shivered
and the dead man swinging from the
branches of a bare tree
was cold when I found him,
very cold indeed.

I touched him.
I knew him.
All day long my hands
smelled of him.

That's how it is.

And when you reached for me later
I wasn't there.
When you touched me again
I was nowhere.

I don't know where you go
but when you are gone
the animal that I am
lies down and is silent.

The world is white,
small. I can't live in it.
It takes you away.
You choose to go
where you know I cannot follow.

There is no choice.
We take from each other
what can never be shared

I rise, you rise,
into the empty arms of morning.

GONE

The door closes
and then you are nowhere.
I try to follow but
all doors open inwards and
you are not anywhere.

Somewhere in the darkness
you are waking

and when I come running
it is to hold you
I want to hold you.

The streets are empty
I am running towards you
towards something I don't know

I can't stop
can't wait to touch you

but the door opens
and then I am not anywhere.

Somewhere I am walking
and the dream has no ending

above me, all clouds and stars,
the sky has no beginning.

It is like this in the evening,
when we wake together;

lying still
our bodies are certain

we are seasons with no names
embracing all weathers.

Your breath on my lips is dry,
is burning.
You remember that thirst
like the first time you
tasted water.

We drove through an old rain
after not speaking for a week.
I cried when you left

cried and cried for the words
not said.

We never believed in them.
Father, lover, we were stranded,
were islands.

Your daughter rode towards us on a
horse. Your daughter who walks
like me, with a slight stoop,

and cries, too, when you leave her.

"& the great white horses come up
  & lick the frost of the dream"

I touch your cold face,
your closed lips and eyes.
I touch the dead place in the
bed, the place where you still lie.

"Did you remember to feed the horses?"
you say, suddenly rising.

Of course the horses.

You dreamed   they died.

we went out walking.
I was a whole new world inside,
alive and bending.

You picked thimbleberries,
one for each finger.
Nimble, we mended.

Something, not death, is faithful.

"AND ON THE COMING OF THE OUTRAGEOUS DAWN"

I want you to
come to my bed,
I don't know you.
I know your eyes– they
depend on the sea. I don't
believe in a language
that brings us closer together.

I want you to be gentle
because the world is wild.
The cool light of the moon
can look on weakness and
never falter.
I've seen you in darkness
defying the moon's skill.
You remain whole and golden.

I want you to
come to my bed, I want you to
come slowly. Forget what you
left or why I returned,
forget that we ever were lonely.

Holding you is like
letting something go;
knowing this, I need you.
Now your eyes reach for me,
join us, speak of children.
Turning to you, I embrace them.

VI

MY BOOTS DRIVE OFF IN A CADILLAC

MY BOOTS DRIVE OFF IN A CADILLAC

Always when I am dreaming
my boots, with my socks inside them,
drive off in a Cadillac
and I have to go barefoot
looking for nightlife.

The car has California plates—
I'll never forget it.
I'll never forget those boots, either.
They were handtooled in Italy.

They were always too big for me,
they slipped off easily.
I never did think they were meant for me.
They were made for someone who was
far less flighty.

The socks had a special significance,
they were given to me by a sailor.
They were a size too small but he
wanted me to wear them.
He wasn't what you'd call a sophisticated
person.

I don't know what it symbolizes,
this dream where nothing fits properly.
It's almost as if I were going around naked
or, worse, with no body at all
to make the old men wet their lips and ogle.

The men think they can buy me.
Up and down the strip I walk with a
hard line for takers— I'm no bargain.
I'm looking for a good time, a change

won't do it.
I'm dreaming of something more than a change
when my boots drive off in a Cadillac.

The corpse was dressed in the
back seat of the car and
I couldn't resist– I kissed him.
Right away he sat up; I could
feel his heart quicken through the
hot silk of his shirt.

My husband was asleep in the
front seat at the wheel. He is a
holy man given to easy women.
I am quite easy myself these days,
giving myself freely and for
no good reason.

This isn't a confession.
The sun was coming up and the
corpse too, for light and air,
for another shot of cognac, and,
if I'm honest, a closer look
at my cleavage.

It was the 5:30 ferry and we
were the only passengers. My
husband was reading the scriptures;
my scruples, you might say, were
about to be compromised.

The corpse was unbuttoning and
I was inclined to watch, when off
Beaver Point a fleet of blackfish
surfaced. They swam towards us like
undertakers out of the mist and
surrounding the boat they shouldered it.

Like a coffin we were carried
out beyond the islands. My husband

prayed – a calm man in a storm – while
the corpse got dressed again and
I grew increasingly silent.

For the whales, I heard them,
were singing – of their past lives
or our lives brief in passing –
I'll never know which for there
they left us stranded.

My husband prayed for wind while
the corpse and I resumed foreplay,
less earnestly than before with
an empty bottle between us.

When back into the mist, as
things will, the whales went,
black sails growing slack and
finally invisible.

I remember afterwards that the
sea stayed calm, blood calm for days
and the kelp gulls cried over us.
But always late at night we could
hear that ghostly song.
The words floated back to us like
wreaths over the gulf.

"CONVERSATION DURING THE OMELETTE AUX FINES HERBES"

I met a dead man walking in the woods today,
myself a healthy woman, barely twenty-seven.
His breath smelled of white wine and wild
strawberries– the finest white wine and the
ripest fruit.

It was intoxicating.
Our dogs gambolled together,
one black and the other white.
I told him the story of my whole life,
as far back, that is, as I chose to remember.
He wanted to know if I would be his wife–
I said under the circumstances
that would be impossible.

We reached the road that led to my house–
he kissed me, very gently.
He wanted to take me all the way,
after another kiss I agreed and invited him in
for a small meal and some light music.

One kiss more and I was on the floor
when who should walk in but my husband,
a horticulturist.
He had a cauliflower from the garden
he wanted to show me but when he saw us lying there
he said *your dog is in the garbage*
fighting with another dog

I just thought I'd mention it.

My dead man revived quite quickly,
aroused by being caught in such a compromising position.

I assured him my husband abhorred all forms of violence
and poured us each a stiff drink in the drawing room.

Your wife tells me you enjoy gardening,
our guest says, as I slip off into the kitchen to make
a good cheese sauce for my husband's cauliflower.
Small talk has never interested me
particularly.

A hunchback followed me home
with an armload of black tulips,
a black hunchback with a waxed moustache–
he must have been a magician.

I say that because it was the wrong season
for tulips. The ground was covered with
leaves and just breathing I walked quickly;
the shadows were gathering like cutthroats
in the ditches.

Inside the house I felt safe from all
things though there were petals under my
covers, messages in my dreams. I think
because I missed you I noticed these things
so much. When you were asleep beside me it was
more than just enough.

But the hunchback had followed me in, it was
not an illusion. He was naked so I gave him
one of your suits, the one you never wore
that was covered with little stars.

The house suddenly changed; it felt colder
and I was a stranger. Even when he was gone
he still possessed me– I use the word possessed
because without him there was nothing left of me.

I threw out the black tulips. They smelled
of flesh, old flesh both fish and reptile,
and I think they finally died at the
bottom of the garden. I can't get rid of the
smell, it may be something permanent. You will

notice it when you come back, months from now,
in your white suit cut to perfection.

You will notice the scars, too, when we are
both finally naked. In the darkness split by
lightning our nakedness should be clear to us,
but love could be there to comfort us
through the bursts of dirty thunder.

IT'S EASY TO BE SLEAZY

Orphans and widowers
they are my weakness.
Soldiers and Indians–
I've a soft spot for criminals.

They're the same after dark –
it's true – I envy them.
I could never be a lesbian
it's far too subliminal.

If I were a man
I could be a rapist.
I'd want to be obvious.
It sounds outrageous.

If you want the truth of it,
that's the thrust of it.
Love may be dead in us
but lust flourisheth.

I feel it like a disease
in the presence of my physician.
My dentist probes with confidence,
my lawyers are more reticent.

Sooner or later I'd have them all–
a pelvic missionary, I'd explore
the deepest regions of my
unexploited territories.
I'd even have time for an
animal or two, not to mention
the natives.

It's purely carnal–

there's nothing romantic about it.
Come on over to my place later
we'll have a few drinks, slip into
something more comfortable you know
and . . . talk about it.

Peter M. was a bit acrobatic
for my taste. He stood on his head,
did tricks in bed to please me.
It didn't do much. I left him.

I was living with George anyway.
We went to Le Touquet with Lord Lucan
and spent an amusing weekend
gambling and so on.

I left them there eventually
and took off to Ireland
(men being my main weakness)
to visit the poet Richard Murphy.

John Berryman, this is for you.
I didn't know you and I don't drink much
but I lie awake sometimes and read your poetry.
I think I know how you feel, or felt.
I feel the same way a lot of the time myself.

I had a drink with George the other night.
I think he's envious of you.
That's all there is in the end, John.
George is the jealous type.

TABOO-MAN

He is fast and keeps bees
drives a flashy car
a widow on each knee

takes me voodoo-dancing
in dreams
paints his body with signs

tattoo-man

takes a hard line
ties knots in my shadow

bully-boy

I give him meat on a hook
bad blood and a butcher's curse.

I only lift up my skirt,
he grows old and mentally crippled.

I offer asylum,
I conserve spittle.
Still he wants a woman made in
somebody else's image.

I will strip naked in graveyards,
leave my body and
fly off

I will voodoo-dance in a
shallow grave
singing my own song
I will rage, rage, rage.

Taboo-man
lends me his hand

I want to marry him,
wear swamp-dock to the altar.

He wants to hurt,
likes cold women only.
Dames to rub dust into his
old wounds, old babes to
crucify him over and over.

Ju-ju man judges beauty by the
number of scars,
love by the persistence of the
infection.

Hocus-pocus man
I want your glass eye,
your good eye, too

mumbo-jumbo man
I want order.

I want dancing in my body
all down my broken body

I want to litter the beaches
with bones

long white bones of happiness
and laughter.

I want to rave.
I want to moan.

Taboo-man
I believe in you
taking and forsaking
love like you do.

I've slept for days in the same clothes
in Mrs. King's new bungalow.
I don't see any reason to change–
the mind might get lost in the process.

I've been dreaming most of the time–
I've dreamed about men who are
perfectly formed and naked.
There's no chance of meeting any of those types
around here– Mrs. King keeps a clean house
and more's the pity.

Ken S. says I don't like men–
he obviously doesn't understand my poetry.
He teaches English at a respectable institution
and reviews a bit.

Mrs. King won't read the papers–
that way, she says, she keeps out of trouble.
I don't blame her, it's just that I'm curious.
Ken says I don't like sex, either.

Mrs. King thinks I'm crazy–
I've slept in the same clothes for days.
If I stripped like those around me
she'd think I was making progress.
I feel more natural when I'm dressed this way.

I won't live in her house much longer,
I can picture myself in another location.
Maybe I'll give notice tomorrow.
Mrs. King will be hurt– there's no solution.

Ken says I'm fickle; I've always been the same.
I mean, I need a new man, an excuse to change.

None of that for Mrs. King–
she only had one husband.
Still she considers him a good investment–
he died suddenly.

Last night in a dream I made love to various men.
When I woke up I found Ken
making notes for a scholarly article.
He's no competition– he can't perform.
He has entered the event when
the dance is already over.

COCKTAILS AT THE MAUSOLEUM

A name may be glorious but death is death
– Richard Eberhart

I decided long ago that death
was not serious, if we went
anywhere else it would be less curious.
So I rode into the woods with
an outlaw and his errand-boy
and drank, and made a lot of noise,
at some rich man's mausoleum.

Others had been before, revellers,
to the same place, with little care
for the monument, a vulgar Parthenon.
Of course it was out of place in
those woods, but so were we–
I would have preferred a comfortable bed
but when you ride into the arms
of an outlaw, you lie anywhere.

We lay down together.
I'm afraid the fear had gone out of me,
valuable and available I long ago
had given up my rich husband
preferring to live, if necessary, disreputably.

Here lies so and so I read, turning
my head to breathe the crushed leaves
damp beneath the ghostly boot-heels:
he is dead. I heard ice-cubes clink
in a glass and somebody stirring. You said
there are reasons for death
and proposed a toast to the living.

Oh, it's easy to sniff
but I did not notice when the errand-boy

slipped away, nor my own glass growing empty
while I drank nothing. I was
thinking of love spent, and grief that
gropes slowly like a tendril, gnarled and
clutching over the enormous years.

Here lies so and so, his name
moss-covered though perhaps, to some,
still glorious. I decided long ago
that death was not serious, but now
with a jewelled hand something tugged,
and I felt the cold earth
rising to meet me.

It's no matter. All my life I had been
waiting for a sign, for death, too,
because I was born wanting. *There are*
good reasons for death, you said,
and sucked the spicy liquor from my
last small breath.

down along the old canal
wearing an ankle-length overcoat
in spite of the heat

sucking sweets by Appointment
To Her Majesty–
the old girl got a good kick
out of that one.

You should have seen her
doing a gang-scuffle outside the
dancehall
or perfuming her body in one of the
lavatories:

she was perfect.

She dressed for the occasion,
a crowbar up her skirt and a
quantity of quicklime.
Hard luck to the whore found dead
in a weedbed

she was queen of the quick throw
queen of alley ways.

She was beautiful and we
loved her

pock-marked with a pistol
she danced naked over our faces

queen of the underground

it felt good, good, good
to be lying beneath her.

They all loved her,
the tarts and muggers on the
commercial road.
She had a full heart for a
hatchet-man, a kiss for a killer.

You should have seen her
teetering on spikes

a grudge-bearing scullion she was
obvious royalty.

When she danced we came alive,
when she danced she was really living.

There was no dance she couldn't do,
hard and fast in a small lifetime.

JUST LUST

It was
only just

you were chinless
famous
shutters clicked as we
kissed

I saw the photographs afterwards
and I was barely visible.

I don't make a point
of hobnobbing with royalty

it was just lust
I said, I'm a married woman
anyway.

Flustered by my common touch
you fumbled for my knee

the travelling spotlights paused,
you coughed

the orchestra played
God Save the Queen.

is perhaps black.
There's a fault, a crack–
nothing is appeasable

our eternal shortness of existence
ensures it.

The heart is functional,
a performer. Its shadow
eschews respectability
sings blues, sings blues

The Black Saint and the Sinner Lady
a split audience of two

heart, a tired waltz
shadow, a jazz funeral.

I got rhythm
I got rhythm

That's my nigger!
That's my nigger!

the eggs were rolling in.
I counted the dead, the newly hatched.
Slate-grey they were prey for the
lice-seized vultures.

You were proficient on the harmonica.
I was an amateur baritone.
We entertained those turtles all night
– female turtles mostly –
with a gay accordion medley.

The turtles were in a trance–
they slashed seaward.
We partied until dawn
composing tight verses to disembowelled
farm-workers of both sexes.

William wrote a sonnet–
he was really a minor poet.
Maggie Laird played a bad violin solo:
her missing limbs can be found in
Los Angeles.

VII

YOU DIDN'T FIT

ONE MORE LYRIC, ONE MORE

For Patrick Lane

I fail, we all fail—
that's the morality of it.
We don't know how to love,
we make a career of it.

Richard says I write in symbols,
Patrick smashes another glass.
Poetry has never been anything
but trouble. We hurt because of it.

The glass cuts; Richard says
blood is symbolic.
I say it's real.
Wounds don't heal; scars are evidence.

We don't know how to die,
we make an art of it.
Patrick says we're in trouble anyway,
it's Winnipeg, it's winter.

We don't have much to say,
words betray pain.
It's late. There's snow.
In bars up the Coast we cursed the rain.

"I DO NOT KNOW IF THINGS THAT HAPPEN CAN BE SAID TO COME TO PASS OR ONLY HAPPEN"

but another year has passed
and the change is marked.
Right from the start my life stopped
making sense

at the core there was only terror,
a compass of blood in the heart's
wreckage and blood and more blood
in every direction.

It spilled out of me,
there was no reason.
As a child I buried everything
I loved, buried it down deep
and seemed pleased.

Years later the doctors
dragged it up,
opened me inside and cut the
stubborn mother from my womb.

My father rocked in his chair
unable to share his last breath
with anyone.
That was years ago when we
thought he wouldn't live much longer.
He still drives down the highway
to see me.

Ten years ago I spent Christmas
in a locked ward.
Some of my best friends
had already committed suicide.

I tried too but it wasn't in me.
The terror went deeper
where nothing could reach me.
I fell in love easily
and for no reason.
I still think, even now, I could be
more discriminating.

Another year has passed,
a decade.
Walking on New Year's Day
with friends who have survived
like me, by accident
– there is something to be said
for having such friends –
I think of the choices we made
along the way, how things
came to pass, or happened,
what brings us finally together.

The years will make sense of it.
Deeper into the shadows
where the patient trees endure
and grow, a small bird rises up
out of our silence, crying
shy and wild towards open water.

YOU DIDN'T FIT

For my father

You wouldn't fit in your coffin
but to me it was no surprise.
All your life you had never fit in
anywhere; you saw no reason to
begin fitting now.

When I was little I remember
a sheriff coming. You were
taken to court because your
false teeth didn't fit and you
wouldn't pay the dentist. It was
your third set, you said none of them
fit properly. I was afraid then
that something would take you from me
as it has done now: death
with a bright face and teeth that
fit perfectly.

A human smile that shuts me out.
The Court, I remember, returned
your teeth, now marked an exhibit.
You were dismissed with costs—
I never understood. The teeth were
terrible. We liked you better
without them.

We didn't fit, either, into your
life or your loneliness, though you
tried, and we did too. Once
I wanted to marry you, and then left;
I'm still the child who won't fit
into the arms of anyone, but is
always reaching.

I was awkward for years, my bones
didn't fit in my body but stuck out
like my heart– people used to comment
on it. They said I was very good
at office parties where you took me
and let others do the talking – the
crude jokes, the corny men – I saw
how they hurt you and I loved you
harder than ever.

Because neither of us fit. Later you
blamed me, said "You must fit in"
but I didn't and I still think
it made you secretly happy.

Like I am now: you won't fit in your
coffin. My mother, after a life
of it, says, "This is the last straw."
And it is. We're all clutching.

The dog had been shut in the
house all day;
we were talking about love, how
sometimes it happens that you are
loved and then you are
not loved. *I'd leave him*,
you said, meaning
him, the man I love;
it's difficult, sometimes, confusing.

The dog had been shut in the
house for days.
We were talking about possibilities, how
sometimes it happens that you are
friends and then you are
not friends. *I want to*,
I said, meaning
you this time. *I told you so*,
you said; we went to bed
and the dog watched.

Years later when we woke
our families had forgotten us,
our friends had almost forgiven us.
We had children of our own,
a life where nothing else mattered.
Love, the possibilities, seemed
somehow unattainable.

You walk out later still; it is a
cold morning.
You forgot the dog, I said.
The dog is dead.

I killed a cucaracha.
I did it instinctively as if some
arbitrary act was necessary.
I needed proof that you had left–
your absence wasn't enough. I suppose
you could say the gesture was symbolic
but this seems too obvious and
you know me better than that.

You said you'd be gone for less than
an hour but it seems to me whole seasons
have passed. The blood of the cucaracha
has dried. I covered the stain with your
new pair of shoes – cowardly, you might say,
to conceal the act.

It's complicated sometimes.
Endings are not innocent, but neither
is love or suffering. You left early,
you'll come back late. The fact that I
recently killed something will begin
to seem irrelevant.

Perhaps I won't tell you and we'll
deal with the blood in the morning.
Tonight we'll hold each other
needing only that. We'll make love
instinctively as if some
mutual act is necessary. "This is love,"
you will whisper. I'll remember it.

I WAS EATING LUNCH ALONE
IN A CLAM BAR IN NEW YORK

when a cat came in wearing
a rat necklace.
I was in the middle of my
second week
of remembering what it felt like
to be lonely, when suddenly
I caught a scent that reminded me
of France.

The cat walked in, just in time,
upset everybody's stomach
but mine. I went out into
the street, into the rain that was
always falling, and for
the next few minutes I was
oblivious, omnipotent.

When I got home you phoned, asked
when was I coming back. I smiled
and looked at the cat, I said
you ought to see this cat, he is
wearing a rat necklace.
He followed me.

I stroked the cat, thinking of your
warm body in bed; the cat purred
and made much of the situation– after all
he was an outcast.

Then suddenly I was afraid, and
hung up the phone. I put the cat outside
because I wanted to love nothing,
and his scent reminded me

of a trip we'd taken to France.
We'd held each other, and we'd danced.

In the morning I found the cat,
headless outside my door.
The rats wanted their freedom too,
and they got it.

ON BEING TOLD, TEN YEARS AGO,
NEVER TO USE THE WORD "TIME" IN A POEM

I have eaten my glass clock.
It ticked too loudly beside the
bed where I, sleeping lightly, dreamed
of the words you left me with,
little keepsakes.

I want to call you brother
but you are other than that.
When you went away I found
my body infested with stars;
on each breast hungered a moon
and my eyes became hours
consuming the doubts of sour men.

I held my breath while the clock
wound down, but the days passed and
your letters, little bloodhounds,
found me. You loved me back;
we kept each other living.

That was the crime,
the act of letting it happen.
So when I try to recall your face,
your warm body in bed,
the clock sounds like goodbye.

It cries inside me where the
stars once raged, ragged pieces of
glass becoming part of me.
Pain thinks it can alter me but
that time has passed. Without you
I have made of love
what time cannot outlast.

I AM NOT A CONSPIRACY
EVERYTHING IS NOT PARANOID
THE DRUG ENFORCEMENT ADMINISTRATION IS
NOT EVERYWHERE

Paul comes from Toronto on Sunday
to photograph me here in my
new image. We drive to a cornfield
where I stand looking uncomfortable.
The corn-god has an Irish accent—
I can hear him whispering, "Whiskey!"

And the cows. They, too, are in the
corn, entranced like figures in effigy.
Last summer in Mexico I saw purses at the
market made from unborn calfskin—
I've been wondering where they came from
ever since, the soft skins I ran my hands
down over, that made me feel like shuddering.

I was wrong. The corn-god is whispering
"Cocaine!" He is not Irish, after all,
but D.E.A. wanting to do business. He
demands to know the names of all my friends,
wants me to tell him who's dealing.

I confess I'm growing restless as the
camera goes on clicking, standing naked in the
high-heel shoes I bought last summer in Mexico.
"We want names," say the cows, who suddenly
look malevolent. They are tearing the ears
off the innocent corn. They call it an
investigation.

Paul calls to them, "Come here, cows!"
though I don't even want them in the picture.
What Paul sees is something different from

me; my skin feels like shuddering when those
cows run their eyes down over me.

"But didn't you smuggle this poem into Canada?"
asks the cow with the mirrored sunglasses.
"As far as we can tell, this is not a
Canadian poem. Didn't you write it
in Mexico?"

I was everything at once,
fish, line and lure
and small boat with person adrift in it.
I'd even go so far
as to say I was the sea.

I should describe how it felt
to be a fish pulling itself in
hooked through its own heart
by something inseparable from its flesh.

I felt confused. I felt uncertain.
When the boat rocked, I rocked too,
and when the sea turned greasy and dark
I had to roll, I was one with it.

At times I had human thoughts,
I wanted to reel in the fish and eat it.
At other times I sympathized with the sea;
I wanted to beach the boat or scuttle it.

Talk about being in two places at once–
I was in six at least. I was cold, too,
irritable in my skin and unnatural
at the end of the line. Yet, understand me,
I knew how it felt to be that line,
taut and purposeful, baited in fate's hand.

It must have been you
in your little aluminum boat
who came zigzagging through a squall to
bring me to my senses. Six of them
adrift in a body with teeth chattering and

mind teetering on the brink of a
horizon which, you pointed out,
wasn't really there. You said the world
was round, not square. *Good news*, I thought,
and started rowing.

Last night I sat in my bath
staring at the wallpaper.
The wallpaper was peeling and
I was thinking that if my bath had been
in Colombia or even Australia
there would have been cockroaches
watching me, watching me thinking
of you as I soaped my body staring
at the wallpaper

which was peeling.
Cockroaches are the worst sorts
of voyeurs. They don't see properly.
And I was thinking of you
on sabbatical in Australia
unable to write because of cockroaches
drawn to the blank sheet in your
typewriter, perhaps because of the light.

And I thought as I sat in
total darkness, the candle having
burned out

I don't blame them—
I'm drawn, too.
To the clean sheet, the mysteries.
This is one of those poems
for you.

NOTES ON POEMS

I have written notes on many of these poems in the way that I might introduce them at a poetry reading: this gives them a context, I feel, without attempting to explain them away.

PART I

Paul and the Full Moon: Acapulco, July 1980. There was a U.S. destroyer anchored in the harbour in front of our house and each night the rains came, the thunderstorms. The small pool on the patio overflowed, mangoes fell from the trees and we had to sleep under dampened sheets to keep ourselves cool. One night it cleared and there was a full moon.

The Plane Put Down in Sacramento: Two weeks before leaving Canada, in July 1980, I had a dream of flying to Sacramento and taking a bus into the foothills, the way I'd done every summer when I was a child, to visit my godmother. After I woke up I wrote the poem, and it was another of those prophetic dream/poem sequences because soon afterwards I found myself on a plane flying over Sacramento (we didn't actually land, but some deviation from the dream is permitted) to Mexico City. Paul and I took a bus, The Dolphin Line, out to the coast. Not into the desert, as in the dream; again, there was a slight deviation.

The Moon Is Upside Down in the Sky: In Acapulco there were frogs that made a sound like a cross between a duck and a goat. I found one sitting inside the gates of a great hacienda; he had been mummified by the heat. In Northwest Coast Indian cultures the frog is a symbol of, among other things, transformation, fertility, magic – for women, in particular. Barbeau writes that, among the Tlingit, the frog crest was the crest of a "secret society belonging exclusively to women." I had on, the whole time we were in Latin America, my own trinity: a Haida frog bracelet made by Gordon Cross of Skidegate, a frog ring from the Shetland Islands on my right-hand middle finger, and a gold pre-Columbian frog from Bogota around my neck (eventually stolen from a drawer in my hotel room on Contadora, the luxury resort off the coast of Panama where the Shah of Iran spent some time in exile). I learned from my friend Johnny Jesus in Panama, that in some parts of Latin America the frog is a symbol for an informer, that *sappo* means *squealer,* and that, when he first met me, he assumed I must be working for the U.S. Drug Enforcement Administration. In Mexico, Panama, and Colombia, I was away from so much that was familiar. It is hard to replace images of cedar-bark, salal and salmonberry bushes with papayas, mangoes and avocados.

Coming into Town, Cold: After a while in Miami (Spring 1981), where I used to lie awake at night listening to the palm fronds brushing the window and wishing it were rain instead, northern rain, we moved to Panama. I wrote this poem in my room at the Hotel Continental, still feeling homesick for Canada. I was struggling with Spanish, taking a course at the YMCA in the Canal Zone, a course for house-wives mainly, married to men in the U.S. Forces. *"¡Estas ollas! ¡Qué bonitas! ¡Como brillan!"* ("These pots! How pretty! How they shine!") I took a taxi to my class the first day and the black driver made lewd suggestions in the rear-view mirror. I told him, in the little Spanish I knew, that my wife played the piano very well. He must have thought I was crazy, because he left me alone after that.

Taking You to the Airport: I stayed alone, during the rainy season, in an apartment with bars on the doors and windows, where it was so humid that the Cuban posters we'd had framed to cover the bare walls, fell off and crashed onto the marble floor during the middle of the night.

Hunchback on the Buga Road: Buga (pronounced *Booga*) is a town in southwestern Colombia, north of Cali. One day we rented a car and drove through the mountains, and the wildflowers we found growing there along the edges of the jungle were the kinds that people in northern latitudes spend years cultivating in greenhouses.

Cali: We rented an apartment here, with a view of Christ (a 50-foot statue on the mountain, illuminated at night), the canyon, and the river.

Sir Lionel Luckhoo, Listed in the Guinness Book of Records *as the World's Most Successful Advocate with 228 Successive Murder Acquittals, Humbly Lays His All at the Feet of Jesus:* In 1979 I went to George-town, Guyana, where my friend Christopher Brown was working for the Department of External Affairs. Christopher threw a cock-tail party in our honour (the Red Cross provided the food and the Army an awning in case it rained) and one of the distinguished guests was Sir Lionel, who had been one of Jim Jones's lawyers and who claimed to know the truth about Jonestown, though he would never divulge it for fear of being unable to practise law again in

Guyana. Or live there, or anywhere else, for that matter. After Jonestown, Sir Lionel became a Born-Again Christian, and the title of this poem is taken from his autobiographical note, found on the back of his pamphlet entitled, "To My Muslim Friends."

Ordinary People: This is a poem for Jacobo Timerman, who spent two years in an Argentinian prison. He wrote a book called *Prisoner Without a Name, Cell Without a Number* and came to speak at an Amnesty International Conference in Toronto. Patrick Lane met him there and Timerman told him that when he was a prisoner one of the few books he received was a copy of Liv Ullman's *Changing*. The book had a devastating effect on him in that it reminded him of a world where there was tenderness and compassion and understanding. After he got out of prison he couldn't touch a book of poetry without starting to shake.

The Unconsidered Life: I wrote this after a writer I knew committed suicide. I don't know whether or not I agree with the last line, never having been able to take a stand on either suicide *or* pornography. But in this case I let the poem have its own way. Still, the opinions expressed are not necessarily those of the writer.

Hurt Birds, Vultures, and B-52's: Every time I came back to Canada from Latin America friends would criticize me for not having a suntan. After all, when most people go to the tropics, they come back brown. So, on my last trip back to Panama I decided to go to the beach. To get there we had to drive through the military zone and were greeted by a very large sign: "Warning: Shark-Infested Water." My friends went in swimming; I put on my sun-screen and lay down (after cleaning myself a space amid the cigarette butts and beer bottle caps and used condoms), and looked up at the clean sky. A layer of vultures, high up, circled the beach; above them, six B-52's, camouflaged, were coming in for a landing. I thought of how difficult it was to write anything but political poetry in Latin America, and how self-indulgent all my love poems, poems about relationships, seemed. Bruce Cockburn, after a trip to Nicaragua, wrote, "Some people never see the light / Till it shines through bullet holes."

The Shark Came Up: The night after I got back from the beach (sunburned) I had a dream that a huge shark's tooth came up out of the water, chasing me. I wrote this poem and, by mistake, left it on the dining room table. No one wanted to go to the beach with me again after that.

PART II

"He Only Wishes They Would Hear Him Sing": The title is a line from a poem by Stevie Smith. I went back to Cleggan, in the west of Ireland, in 1978, and found that my landlord was in the hospice in Clifden, dying. This was very irritating because I couldn't stay in the house I had always rented. His son and daughter were staying there, having come a great distance. Everyone wanted Conrad to "go," but he kept hanging on. I had to go myself, but not in that ultimate sense, to Claddaduff where I took up lodgings in Mrs. King's new bungalow.

Eaglet Tricks: In 1975 I spent some time at the Ilkley Theatre Festival in Yorkshire, involved in a production of Ted Hughes' *Cave Birds*, directed by George MacBeth. These poems worked their way into my brain and the only way I could find my own voice again was to make a kind of collage, which this poem is, of Hughes' imagery. I actually hear it being read in his voice, with its sinister Yorkshire accent.

A Tree Wouldn't Just Uproot Itself: I stopped writing poetry (with the exception of this one) during the time I was pregnant. All the clichés about being pregnant were true; I was "biologically fulfilled" and had no need to sublimate my tendencies in verse. As John Fowles says in *Daniel Martin*, "We write out of what we lack, not what we have."

Three Witches Go for Lunch in Elora: This was written in the fall of 1983, when I moved to Ontario to be Writer-in-Residence at the University of Waterloo. Over the next year another seven barns were burned down until finally the person who started the fires was caught – the local fire-chief's son.

PART III

"We Come This Way But Once": This sequence was written while on a poetry reading tour of England, Wales, Scotland, and Paris with George Johnston and bill bissett in the fall of 1980. Every day we got up, caught a train, and went to a new venue. We spent a lot of time on trains, and the rhythm of trains started finding its way into all of our poetry. I think we all wrote something during this trip. The title of this series comes from a cartoon that appeared in *The New Yorker*. A tired man comes home to his tired wife, saying, "I heard some good news today. We come this way but once."

Part i: We talked a lot about our lives. When the trip was over we'd be going our separate ways, bill up to the Cariboo to look for work, me down to Latin America to start another new life, and George back to his close, large family. bill wouldn't let himself have a cigarette until five o'clock everyday, hence the line "in two hours I can smoke." Mrs. Jackson ran a guest house where we stayed near Lumb Bank in Yorkshire; it was very cold and bill found a stone pig in his bed. bill and I went to a church of spiritual healing and I got a stigmata on my palm – shaped like a question mark.

Part iv: The quote, "A single sentence will suffice for modern man: he fornicated and he read the papers," is from Camus' *The Fall*.

Part v: In all fairness to George – he *did* dream; only he says he doesn't remember, now, what the dreams were about.

Part vi: It didn't fit into the poem, but in Paris we saw a bookstore that had been bombed by extremists.

In Whitehorse I Wanted You: The line "I've been bawling to adolescents the inscrutable agonies of the dead" is Dylan Thomas's comment when asked about his reading tour of high schools in the United States. The passage italicized in the poem is from Sheila Watson's *The Double Hook*.

PART IV

Vern and Joanne: Dead: Vern, a Volkswagen mechanic who lived at Cape Ball, seven miles up the beach from Tlell, in the Queen Charlotte Islands, and his wife Joanne, left the 'Charlottes in the late seventies and moved to Brother Love's Commune in Seattle. Mike Davis had been down to the commune, and told us about the accident as we were eating a spaghetti dinner at Tlell. There are a few other references in the poem which may need explanation: Vern had fixed my own vw on a number of occasions; Mike had been in Idaho where it was against the law to have in your possession an eagle's feather (eagle feathers are as common as seagull feathers in the 'Charlottes); and Jack Miller had a large collection of Indian artifacts, a result of the walks he took behind the bulldozers that were cutting roads through old Haida village sites. (A year later his wife got "the kid.")

Requiem for Talunkwun Island: Part i is told from the point of view of a Haida ghost returning to the island. In Part ii the ghost recollects his first contact with the whiteman's ships. Joe Tulip, my friend in Skidegate, told me that when the whiteman first came to the Islands, the Haidas from Kiusta who went aboard their ships came back to the village with a report that the whitemen had a bear cooking for them and that they ate maggots. The bear was actually a black man, the maggots, rice. In Part III the ghost recalls the forests that are gone. Part IV is told from the point of view of the ghost's earthly remains – that is, its skeleton, which has been dug up by archaeologists.

PART V

The poems in this section are all love poems, and need little comment. *"Exile Is in Our Time Like Blood"* is a line from a poem by John Berryman. "& the great white horses come up & lick the frost of the dream" I found in one of Charles Bukowski's books. *"And on the Coming of the Outrageous Dawn"* is from a poem by Theodore Roethke. I wrote this poem in England, when I was tutoring a course for the Arvon Foundation at Lumb Bank (1981). A young man in the group was under the mistaken impression that the poem was for him, and for the next year proceeded to bombard me with proclamations of his love, Swiss chocolates, exotic invitations, books, tapes of his own voice, etc. The ending of this poem was unlike any other I'd written in that it seemed to foretell of some "happy" event. I had never considered having children; but two months later, against all odds, I was pregnant. This poem was, and is, for Paul.

PART VI

In this section, dreams were the origin of many of the poems such as *My Boots Drive Off in a Cadillac* (though it is written from the point of view of a prostitute), *Remy in the Bentley, Taboo-Man, Boogeying with the Queen* and *Just Lust.*

"Conversation During the Omelette aux Fines Herbes": The title is a line from a poem called "Eight for Luncheon" by Cynthia MacDonald. I was happily married at the time, but then I got a letter from someone else. I went for a walk and wrote the whole poem in my head. The "someone else," the person from the past, became "the dead man." The last line in this poem owes a lot to E. J. Tribb (17).

John Berryman, This Is for You: Love and Fame by John Berryman is one of my favourite books of poetry. I wrote this after rereading it, feeling I needed to get Berryman's style out of my system.

Mrs. King's New Bungalow: My book of poems, *A Man to Marry, a*

Man to Bury had just been published and, perhaps because of the title, it got a lot of bad reviews, especially from young men who seemed to think I was a rabid feminist. Actually, the title, though very ambiguous, had been generously conceived; I'd been thinking how, traditionally, when a woman married a man the chances were that she'd outlive him, and have to see him buried. One of the worst reviews appeared in *The Canadian Forum*. In it the reviewer said I obviously hated men and found sex disgusting and quoted a phrase out of context to prove his point, a line from a fertility poem I'd written for Dave Godfrey's cows, so that "I rise like a Christmas moon / impaled on the penis bone of a bear" was reduced, to show my horror of sex, simply to "... impaled on the penis...." I read the review just before I flew to Shannon and stayed a week in Mrs. King's new bungalow. While normally I would not be so upset by a review, I found that I had many hours in the small rain to drink Guinness alone and contemplate the injustice. The ending of this poem is a rephrasing of Robert Lowell's "If you mistake the event don't enter the dance" – advice that all critics should follow, I feel.

Cocktails at the Mausoleum: The full Eberhart quote is from his poem "I Walked over the Grave of Henry James." It goes:

> *I crushed a knob of earth between my fingers,*
> *This is a very ordinary experience.*
> *A name may be glorious but death is death,*
> *I thought, and took a street-car back to Harvard Square.*

Boogeying with the Queen: I had a series of dreams about the royal family. (I once read that to dream of the royal family means that you feel socially inferior.) Before I wrote this poem I dreamed I had won first prize in the Princess Anne Look-Alike contest. The title was a result of "mis-hearing" a line in Warren Zevon's "Werewolves of London." I *thought* the line was, "I saw Lon Chaney ju-ju walking with the Queen," and originally I called my poem *Ju-Ju Walking with the Queen*. From there it was an easy step to *Boogeying with the Queen*.

Just Lust: I dreamed I was having dinner with Prince Charles (this was before Lady Di came along) when he leaned over the juice container (it was a very informal dinner), kissed me, and said, "Rita, I luff you," in a German accent. I told him my name was not Rita, woke up, and wrote this poem. Partly it's for all those people who still ask, "Why doesn't your poetry rhyme?" It really does, you just have to work hard to find the rhyme sometimes.

The Shadow of the Heart: Some of the lines in this poem are taken from old jazz songs, including the last two. I've been warned that many people, not just blacks, may find the last lines offensive, but John Mortimer says, in his great autobiography *Clinging to the Wreckage,* "there can't be 'no go' areas in the world of art. The writer who cuts short a line of work for fear of shocking some people, or 'giving offense' is untrue to his calling."

That Night on Turtle Beach: I wrote this after reading an article in the *National Geographic.* The pictures in that magazine are wonderful. But I'm always wishing the text would explode.

PART VII

One More Lyric, One More: I was in Winnipeg giving a poetry reading one winter and went to Patrick Lane and Lorna Crozier's house for dinner. Patrick made a dish we called "Chicken Poet-Creep." We thought this would be a good title for a cookbook of recipes by poets. Patrick and I talked about how unfashionable it was, especially on the West Coast, to write "lyric" poetry, and how both of us were always being accused of doing so. We talked about language, and emphasis, and how the line "I fail" changes according to where you put the stress. (Sean Virgo, when he read this book in manuscript form, said he thought the first line should be, "We fail, we all fail —." I'm still not sure.) Anyway, at about 10:30 the night of the dinner party, Patrick smashed his wine glass and went to bed. I remember thinking how this was about the only poetic statement, lyrical or otherwise, to be made in Winnipeg that winter.

"I Do Not Know If Things that Happen Can Be Said to Come to Pass or Only Happen": The title is from Howard Nemerov's poem "Death and the Maiden." It is one of my favourite poems, and often when I am in this way enamoured of a poem I deliberately write something in the same voice, or vein, as a form of an exorcism. The walk we took was at Mackenzie Bight, on the west side of the Saanich Peninsula, Vancouver Island. The day seemed to mark the beginning of something more than just another year.

You Didn't Fit: When I living in Colombia, I had a dream one night that my father died. I had to bury him in a small cardboard box, and he didn't fit. When I thought about the dream, which left me with an immense feeling of sadness, I realized it was metaphorical more than anything else, although normally I do not interpret my dreams this way. All his life my father had never fit in anywhere. In 1975, when he came to visit me in Ireland, he kept his watch on Pacific Standard Time for the duration, so that at two in the morning he would be sitting up in front of the turf fire saying, "Well, your mother will just be getting home from school now, and making a cup of tea." In a way I admired his stubbornness, though it made life extremely difficult. Because the dream was so real, and the writing of the poem an act which made his death seem final, I have not been troubled by thoughts of his death since, though I had been previously.

I sent this poem to *Saturday Night* and, after a few months got a revision of it back with a letter saying, "How do you like being edited?" My poem was no longer recognizable. Every reference to teeth had been taken out, and so had three of the seven stanzas, while the stanzas that were left had been put into a new order. I turned down the magazine's offer to publish "my" poem for $200. Which proved to me, at least, that I still had scruples.

Sometimes It Happens: For years I was haunted by Brian Patten's poem of the same title. I had a poster of his poem on my wall and would constantly quote it to friends: ". . . and sometimes it happens that you are loved and then you are not loved, and loving has passed." Again this poem is an exorcism.

After You Left: My editor asked why I'd used the word *cucaracha* instead of plain *cockroach*, as I do in the last poem in the book. It just seemed right. "After you left I killed a cockroach" sounds, to me, melodramatic. Besides, *cockroach* doesn't, in this instance, have enough syllables.

I Was Eating Lunch Alone in a Clam Bar in New York: I was feeling very alienated when I wrote this, because the restaurant (it was actually the Courtyard Café in Toronto) filled up with wealthy, smart couples, and I was alone in my old clothes, which were beginning to look shabby. I'd just bought some postcards, and one of them was of a cat with a string of rats around his neck, and I started fantasizing about the scene that would occur if a cat came in wearing a rat necklace.

I Am Not a Conspiracy, Everything Is Not Paranoid, the Drug Enforcement Administration Is Not Everywhere: Paul Orenstein was the photographer. Obviously I felt uncomfortable in the cornfield, far away from the ocean I'm used to being photographed beside.

Adrift: I hadn't written any poems for over a year and a half when Kevin Roberts wrote asking for some work for a new magazine called *True North Down Under*, Canadian and Australian poetry. I sent what I had. A while later I got a hastily scrawled letter back from one of his co-editors, saying, "These are not up to scratch. We want gold. Send original exciting material." I was, of course, depressed. Just at the one time in my life when I needed encouragement! That night I had a dream, about expectations and so on, and in the morning wrote this poem.

Not a Love Poem: I don't know why I used *cockroach* instead of *cucaracha* here, except that "Cucarachas are the worst sort of voyeurs" would not be a line I would ever consider using in a poem.

ACKNOWLEDGMENTS

Poems in this collection have appeared in the following magazines and anthologies:

In Australia: *Helix; Poetry Australia*

In Canada: *Arts Manitoba; Ariel; Aurora: Canadian Writing* 1980; *Benchmarks; The Canadian Forum; Canadian Literature; Cross-Canada Writers' Quarterly; Event; Exile; Gamut; Grail; Poetry Canada Review; Prism International; Queen's Quarterly; Room of One's Own; Toronto Life; Treeline II; True North Down Under; University College Review; Writing*

In the United Kingdom: *Aquarius; Bananas; New Departures; Slow Dancer; Trends*

In the United States: *Negative Capability; South Shore; Three Rivers Poetry Journal*

The poems "Conversation During the Omelette Aux Fines Herbes"; "Requiem for Talunkwun Island"; "I Want to Remember David"; "Vern and Joanne: Dead"; "Josef's Ghost"; "Sleeping Together"; "Boogeying with the Queen"; and "Just Lust" were also included in *Tarts and Muggers: Poems New and Selected* (McClelland and Stewart, 1982).

"Taboo-Man" was first published by Celia Duthie as a broadside, "The Plane Put Down in Sacramento" as a broadside, also, by Bill Hoffer. "Conversation During the Omelette Aux Fines Herbes" appeared as a Sceptre Press pamphlet (England, 1979).

Printed in Canada